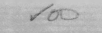

D1499326

Eliot Porter

Eliot Porter

The Grand Canyon

Prestel/ARTnews

Front cover: View up Colorado River, Toroweap, Arizona. August 12, 1969 (plate 52)
Back cover: River-polished schist, Middle Granite Gorge, mile 129.5,
Grand Canyon, Arizona. September 18, 1967 (no. 31 on the map)
Frontispiece: Canyon end in sun, Spook Canyon, Marble Gorge, Grand Canyon,
Arizona. June 16, 1967 (near no. 13 on the map)
Pages 14-15: Map of the Grand Canyon showing the sites photographed by Eliot Porter

Prestel-Verlag, Mandlstrasse 26, D-8000 Munich 40, Germany
Tel. (89) 38 17 09 0; Fax (89) 38 17 09 35

Distributed in continental Europe by Prestel-Verlag,
Verlegerdienst München GmbH & Co KG,
Gutenbergstrasse 1, D-8031 Gilching, Germany,
Tel. (81 05) 21 10; Fax (81 05) 55 20

Distributed in the USA and Canada by te Neues Publishing Company,
15 East 76th Street, New York, NY 10021, USA
Tel. (212) 288 0265; Fax (212) 570 2373

Distributed in Japan by YOHAN-Western Publications Distribution Agency,
14-9 Okubo 3-chrome, Shinjuku-ku, J-Tokyo 169
Tel. (3) 208 0181; Fax (3) 209 0288

Distributed in the United Kingdom, Ireland and all remaining countries by
Thames & Hudson Limited, 30-34 Bloomsbury Street, London WC1B 3QP, England
Tel. (71) 636 5488; Fax (71) 636 4799

ARTnews Associates, 48 West 38th Street, New York, NY 10018, USA
Tel. (212) 398 1690; Fax (212) 819 0394

Designed by Dietmar Rautner, Munich

Typeset by Max Vornehm, Munich
Color separations and printing by Wenschow-Franzis GmbH, Munich
Binding by Conzella Verlagsbuchbinderei GmbH, Aschheim near Munich

Printed in Germany
ISBN 3-7913-1233-2

Contents

Eliot Porter:
A Reminiscence

Beaumont Newhall

Eliot Porter, one of America's foremost photographers, began to photograph as a boy. He had already fallen in love with nature, particularly as he saw it on Great Spruce Head Island, on the coast of Maine, where his family had a summer home. There he took many photographs of birds. "With me," he wrote later, "nature was an undiluted source of pleasure and a reservoir of mysteries that survived and deepened into adult life. Pleasure ultimately found expression in photography, whereas the mysteries of nature called for resolution through knowledge which led me into a career of science."

He graduated from Harvard Engineering School in 1924 with the degree of Bachelor of Science and from Harvard Medical School in 1929. He did not enter the medical profession, but taught bacteriology and biological chemistry from 1930 to 1938. During those years his photography was an avocation.

I first met Eliot Porter in New York in 1938. I was then the librarian of the Museum of Modern Art and acting chairman of its department of photography. One morning a young man came into the library with a portfolio under his arm. He introduced himself and asked if he could show me some photographs. I said "Certainly," and began looking at his excellent prints. Some had been taken in the Austrian Alps, others were landscapes of Maine, and one was a portrait of his infant son.

After lunch he returned. He was jubilant. "Alfred Stieglitz is going to give me an exhibition," he said.

Stieglitz, the champion of photography as an art form, exhibited twenty-nine of Eliot's prints in his New York gallery, An American Place, from December 20, 1938, to January 18, 1939. This was the last show that Stieglitz ever gave a photographer. In the catalogue he wrote: "For four years I have been watching the work of Eliot Porter. In the very beginning I felt he had a vision of his own. I sensed a potentiality. These photographs now shown I believe should have an audience."

The show was well received. Even before it opened, Stieglitz sold seven prints to David McAlpin, a benefactor of the Museum of Modern Art. Stieglitz wrote Eliot: "You'll have to make 40 duplicates." The success of the exhibition meant so much to Eliot that he resigned from his teaching post to make photography his career.

Birds! Birds! Birds! Eliot loved them. He followed them with his camera from the fields to their nests in the forest. He built blinds from which birds could be observed inconspicuously. To capture birds in flight he used the high-speed stroboscopic flashlights that had been specially designed for him by the inventor and photographer Harold Edgerton. Eliot told me that he would set up two or three of these lamps near the birds' nests. The birds learned to fly around them, seemingly undisturbed by the flashes of light.

Eliot hoped that a book could be made of the bird photographs. He showed prints to a publisher, who was impressed by them but regretted that they were black and white. He told Eliot that color was essential to facilitate identification of the birds by their plumage.

So Eliot taught himself the latest technique of color photography. In 1935 the Eastman Kodak Company introduced Kodachrome film that could be used in almost any camera and would produce color transparencies. The processing was done by professional laboratories. Color prints could be made from the transparencies by the photographer himself, using the dye-transfer process. Eliot went back to show the publisher his color prints. This time the publisher turned him down. "The cost of color printing is too great," he said.

In 1960 the George Eastman House in Rochester, New York, showed a splendid exhibition of Eliot's photographs that he titled "The Seasons." It was a collection of color prints with captions taken from the writings of Henry David Thoreau.

Eliot was a guest at the opening of the exhibition. He told my wife, Nancy Newhall, of his disappointment at not being able to find a publisher who would make a book of the entire collection. Nancy had just finished a volume of Ansel Adams's photographs that included her essay "This Is the American Earth." On the spot she telephoned David Brower, the executive director of the Sierra Club, and asked him if the club could publish the book that Eliot envisaged. Brower agreed to the proposal, and the beautiful color prints were published under a new title, taken from Thoreau: *In Wildness Is the Preservation of the World*.

In his final years Eliot traveled widely. Twenty-six books have been published of color photographs taken during his extensive travels from Maine to Colorado, from Africa to the Galápagos, from China to the Antarctic – to name but a few places on his itinerary.

In 1973, while I was a member of the faculty of the University of New Mexico, I gave a course on art museum practices. There were only a few students. We decided to ask Eliot if we could hold an exhibition of his photographs in the University Art Museum. He responded with enthusiasm and invited us to come to his studio in Tesuque to select the prints.

Every Monday for several weeks we spent the better part of the day going through his collection. He stood by at each meeting to answer questions and make suggestions. We hung 288 photographs in the museum gallery. Eighty-five of them were black and white. These included all the prints that had been shown in 1938–39 by Stieglitz.

To our surprise and satisfaction, Eliot gave all the prints to the University of New Mexico in Albuquerque. He often presented the entire contents of exhibitions of his photographs to the museums that had shown them. These include the New Mexico Museum of Fine Arts in Santa Fe, the George Eastman House, and the Amon Carter Museum in Fort Worth, Texas. He was a most generous man, precise in his ways and of great perseverance. He demanded perfection. As a scientist he insisted upon the accuracy of the pictorial record; and he constantly strove to make his pictures meaningful and of lasting value. He was surely a major photographer.

He wrote: "To all the subjects I photographed I apply the criterion that if they were worth recording at all, they are worth doing it in such a way that they can stand repeated viewing, even demand it, so that one can go back again and again to find hidden qualities missed at first. It is always possible to do better, to see more clearly, to translate a clearer vision into a more meaningful and communicative piece of work: this challenge is comforting and sustaining."

Eliot Porter died in Santa Fe on November 2, 1990.

Eliot Porter
and the Grand Canyon

Martin Litton

Each wall of the canyon is a composite structure, a wall composed of many walls, but never a repetition. Every one of these almost innumerable gorges is a world of beauty in itself. In the Grand Canyon there are thousands of gorges like that below Niagara Falls, and there are a thousand Yosemites. Yet all these canyons unite to form one grand canyon, the most sublime spectacle on the earth."

These words are from the journals of John Wesley Powell, who made the first river trip through the Grand Canyon in 1869.

Nearly one hundred years later, Eliot Porter made two trips to the Grand Canyon. He, too, was enchanted by what he saw.

I was a director of the Sierra Club, and I was running tours through the canyon down the Colorado River. There were twelve in the party, including Eliot's son, Patrick, and my son, John. For Eliot, it was a return to the place to which he had been brought by his father as a child, and he was anxious to confirm his early impressions.

We used three wooden boats, called dories, that are guided by oars rather than motors. Motors, I felt, were a travesty of true wilderness experience. The first trip ended 284 miles and seventeen days later.

June is the hottest month in the Grand Canyon. For relief, Eliot and the others would frequently jump overboard and float through minor rapids.

"The sensation is quite unexpected," Eliot wrote. "You suddenly find yourself quietly floating in the river, just drifting along with the current as you bob up and down with the waves. There is no perception of speed until you look at the bank, which you are amazed to see is rushing past. As the lead boat slid into the fast water where the rapid began, it would often appear from the following boats to drop out of sight into a hollow in the river only to reappear a few minutes later on the next crest of water."

Eliot called the canyon a beautiful and awesome spectacle. "Each rapid," he wrote, "is a separate adventure, each has its special thrill. All share in common, however, the excitement provided by the swift glide down the smooth tongue where the river drops off at the head of the rapid and funnels with increasing speed into the first waves, and then by the crash of water over the boat. It is a thrill that never diminishes and which draws people back to the Grand Canyon time and again."

Although he was in his mid-sixties, Eliot, tall and trim, was quite adept at climbing. When we got to a place called Deer Creek, his son helped him with the heavy tripods. There was a little narrow gorge with sheer walls. You couldn't walk in the gorge without walking into the rushing water. You had to be agile. Eliot would go up these walls like a spider – twenty or thirty feet up, scrambling with his camera and gear.

He would set up his camera carefully. He couldn't do that all the time, particularly when we were moving in the boat. Then he would hold the camera in his hand and grab some shots on the fly. He was dazzled by the views. He was always trying to find the best angle to shoot.

There was one accident. One day, the boat was lifted abruptly by a wave with such force that my son, who was twenty at the time, was pitched forward. His leg struck a metal latch causing a five-inch cut that was rather deep.

Eliot was the only member of the party who had a medical degree. We got out our first aid kit, which contained surgical needles. I didn't know the full extent of Eliot's medical experience. He was pulling the wound together with these sutures. I noticed that his hands were shaking. My son was grimacing with pain. I wanted to reassure Eliot, so I said something like, "Eliot, we're certainly lucky you're here to do this." He said, "I don't know why. I've never done this before." I didn't know what to say. My son's teeth were clenched. He was looking at the sky. I said, "Eliot, you've seen it done before." He said, "Only in pictures." Anyway, Eliot performed wonderfully. My son recovered.

One day, many years later, I was sitting with Eliot in his studio in Tesuque, New Mexico, at the edge of the Santa Fe National Forest. At eighty-seven, he was still very active, supervising traveling exhibitions, the publication of new books about his work, and the printing of his photographs. I asked Eliot how he saw himself and his career. "I wanted to make people aware of the natural beauty around them," he said.

Eliot once remarked that the rare photograph, the work of art, was the "creation of love, love for the subject first and love for the medium second." When he was asked to elaborate, he said: "Imogen Cunningham once said to me that she could photograph anything you could put light on. And I think that's a very good statement because it sums it up for me. It doesn't have to be nature, it could be anything. It's how you do it that counts. Every thing in the picture. That's one thing that Alfred Stieglitz told me. When he was criticizing my first pictures, he said, 'It all has to be important.' Every thing in the frame of the photograph has to be important. It has to be a coordinated composition so that it all counts. You can't have false notes. He would criticize my pictures in the beginning when he would put his hand over part of the picture. He didn't really say it, but he indicated that that part doesn't count. It doesn't mean anything."

When I first saw Eliot's transparencies of his Grand Canyon trips, I said to him, "These are tremendous."

Eliot smiled. "Well, it's a tremendous place."

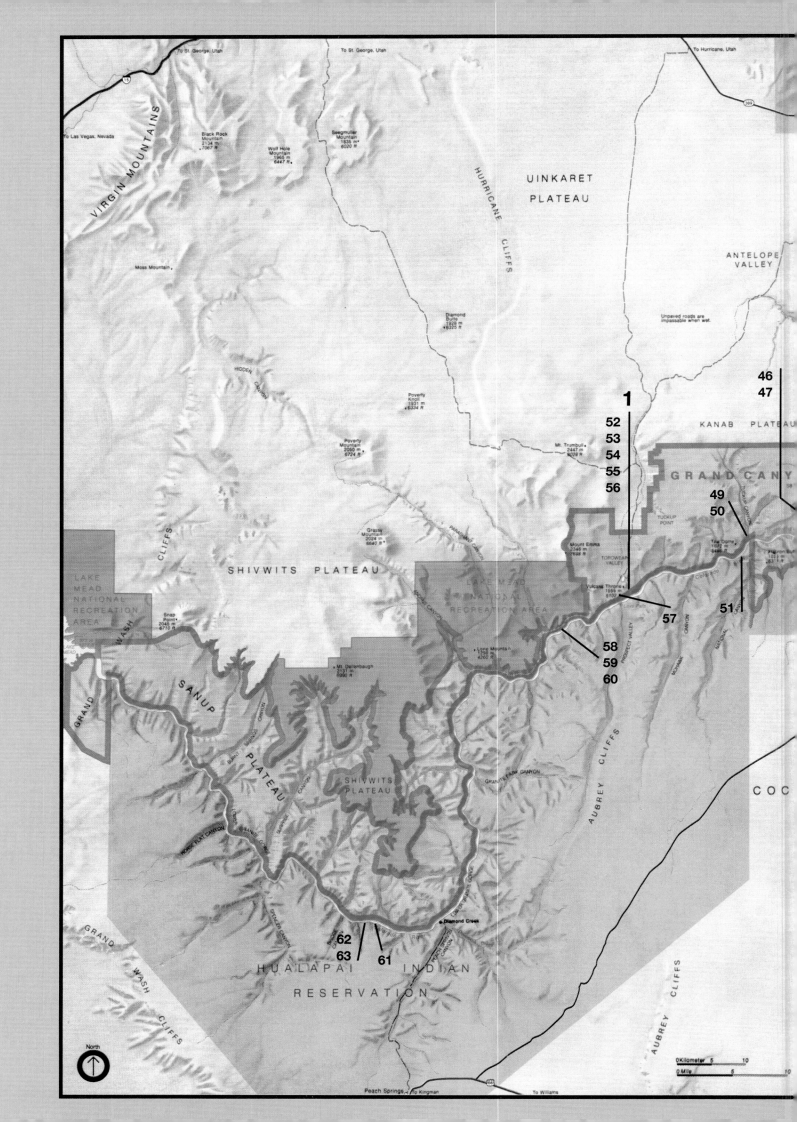

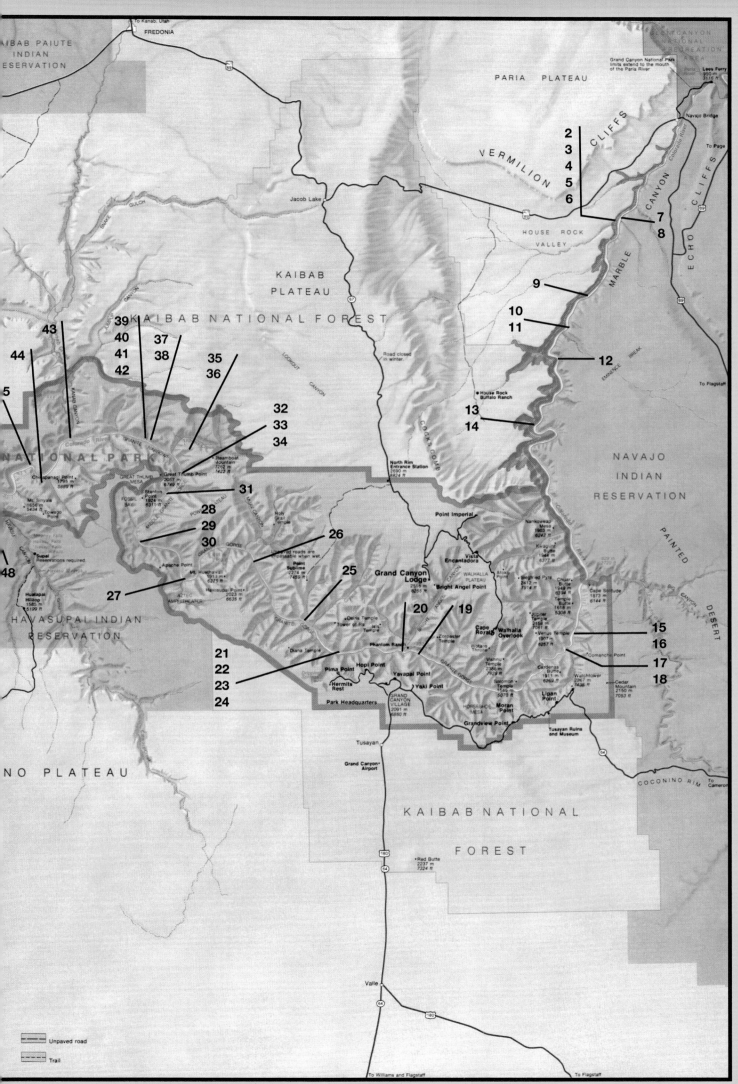

The numbers on the map are those of the illustrations in this book

Acknowledgments

For invaluable assistance
in the production of this book
the publishers would like to thank
Stephen Porter;
Thomas W. Southall, Curator of Photographs,
and Barbara McCandless, Assistant Curator of Photographs,
of the Amon Carter Museum, Fort Worth, Texas;
and the United States Department,
of the Interior, National Park Service,
Grand Canyon National Park,
Grand Canyon, Arizona.

We are also grateful
to Martin Litton
for identifying the sites photographed
on the map
of the Grand Canyon (pp. 14–15).

The Photographs

1

View of Lava Falls,
Toroweap Overlook

GRAND CANYON, ARIZONA
AUGUST 13, 1969

2

Supai ledges,
House Rock Canyon

GRAND CANYON, ARIZONA
JUNE 13, 1967

3

Tamarisk and jimson weed,

House Rock Canyon

GRAND CANYON, ARIZONA

JUNE 13, 1967

4
Mud cracks and pool,
House Rock Canyon

GRAND CANYON, ARIZONA
JUNE 13, 1967

5
Tamarisk and black cliff,
House Rock Canyon

GRAND CANYON, ARIZONA
JUNE 13, 1967

6

Sculptured rock,

House Rock Canyon

GRAND CANYON, ARIZONA

JUNE 13, 1967

7
Rock formations,
upper Marble Gorge to mile 16

GRAND CANYON, ARIZONA
SEPTEMBER 12, 1967

8

Dark rocks at edge of river, mile 16,
above House Rock Canyon

GRAND CANYON, ARIZONA
SEPTEMBER 13, 1967

9
Fluted limestone,
mile 26, Marble Gorge

GRAND CANYON, ARIZONA
SEPTEMBER 13, 1967

10

Wet sand at edge of river,
29-Mile Rapid, Marble Gorge

GRAND CANYON, ARIZONA
JUNE 15, 1967

11

Boulders on edge of river,
29-Mile Rapid

GRAND CANYON, ARIZONA
JUNE 15, 1967

12
Sandbar,
Redwall Cavern, Marble Gorge

GRAND CANYON, ARIZONA
JUNE 15, 1967

13

Reeds and reflections,

Buck Farm Canyon

GRAND CANYON, ARIZONA
SEPTEMBER 14, 1967

14

Buck Farm Canyon

GRAND CANYON, ARIZONA
SEPTEMBER 14, 1967

15
Boulders
in Lava Canyon

GRAND CANYON, ARIZONA
JUNE 17, 1967

16

Cottonwood tree,

Lava Canyon

GRAND CANYON, ARIZONA
JUNE 17, 1967

17

White-tufted beard grass,
Tanner Flat

GRAND CANYON, ARIZONA
SEPTEMBER 14, 1967

18

Tamarisk
and Colorado River

GRAND CANYON, ARIZONA
SEPTEMBER 14, 1967

19

Rock formations
above Bright Angel Creek

GRAND CANYON, ARIZONA
SEPTEMBER 16, 1967

20

Granite wall and boulders,
Bright Angel Creek

GRAND CANYON, ARIZONA
SEPTEMBER 16, 1967

21

Tamarisks and river,
above Granite Falls

GRAND CANYON, ARIZONA
JUNE 20, 1967

22

View up river with boulders,
Granite Falls

GRAND CANYON, ARIZONA
JUNE 20, 1967

23
Boulders and sand dune,
Granite Falls

GRAND CANYON, ARIZONA
JUNE 19, 1967

24

View down canyon with boulders,
Granite Falls

GRAND CANYON, ARIZONA
JUNE 19, 1967

25
Sculptured schist,
Tuna Rapid

GRAND CANYON, ARIZONA
JUNE 21, 1967

26

Edge of sandbar with rock,
above Bass Rapid, mile 106

GRAND CANYON, ARIZONA
SEPTEMBER 17, 1967

27
Waterfall,
Elves' Chasm

GRAND CANYON, ARIZONA
SEPTEMBER 17, 1967

28

Shadow on cliff with reflections,
mile 122

GRAND CANYON, ARIZONA
JUNE 22, 1967

29

Sand dune and
river's edge, green reflections,
mile 122

GRAND CANYON, ARIZONA
JUNE 22, 1967

30

Barrel cactus,
mile 122

GRAND CANYON, ARIZONA
JUNE 22, 1967

31
Middle Granite Gorge,
mile 129.5

GRAND CANYON, ARIZONA
SEPTEMBER 19, 1967

32
View across canyon,
Stone Creek

GRAND CANYON, ARIZONA
JUNE 22, 1967

33
Fan-shaped falls,
Stone Creek

GRAND CANYON, ARIZONA
JUNE 22, 1967

34
Grass and pools,
Stone Creek

GRAND CANYON, ARIZONA
JUNE 22, 1967

35
Small waterfall,

Tapeats Creek

GRAND CANYON, ARIZONA
JUNE 23, 1967

36
Thunder River Falls,
with moss and log

GRAND CANYON, ARIZONA
JUNE 23, 1967

37

Water flowing in the chasm,

Deer Creek

GRAND CANYON, ARIZONA

JUNE 24, 1967

View into the chasm,

Deer Creek

GRAND CANYON, ARIZONA

JUNE 24, 1967

40
Goldenrod, Deer Creek

GRAND CANYON, ARIZONA
SEPTEMBER 19, 1967

41
Reflections in Deer Creek
at river's edge

GRAND CANYON, ARIZONA
SEPTEMBER 20, 1967

42
Reeds and reflections,
Deer Creek mouth

GRAND CANYON, ARIZONA
SEPTEMBER 20, 1967

43

Sand ripples and reflections,
Kanab Creek

GRAND CANYON, ARIZONA
JUNE 24, 1967

44

Matkatamiba Canyon

GRAND CANYON, ARIZONA
JUNE 28, 1967

45
Stones and reflections,
Upset Canyon mouth

GRAND CANYON, ARIZONA
SEPTEMBER 20, 1967

46
Looking into Grand Canyon,
Boysag Point

GRAND CANYON, ARIZONA
AUGUST 17, 1969

47
Jasperized fossils in sandstone,
Boysag Point

GRAND CANYON, ARIZONA
AUGUST 17, 1969

48
River edge and catclaw bush,
below Havasu Creek

GRAND CANYON, ARIZONA
JUNE 26, 1967

49

Large square boulder,

Tuckup Canyon

GRAND CANYON, ARIZONA

SEPTEMBER 21, 1967

51
Limestone chute,

National Canyon

GRAND CANYON, ARIZONA
SEPTEMBER 21, 1967

52

View up Colorado River,

Toroweap Overlook

GRAND CANYON, ARIZONA

AUGUST 12, 1969

53
Canyon wall,

Toroweap Overlook

GRAND CANYON, ARIZONA
AUGUST 12, 1969

54
Canyon edge,
Toroweap Overlook

GRAND CANYON, ARIZONA
AUGUST 12, 1969

56
Narrow side canyon,
near Toroweap Overlook

GRAND CANYON, ARIZONA
AUGUST 13, 1969

57
Lichens and sagebrush roots,
Vulcan's Throne

GRAND CANYON, ARIZONA
AUGUST 13, 1969

Columnar basalt,
above Whitmore Wash

GRAND CANYON, ARIZONA
AUGUST 18, 1969

59
Lava flow with vegetation,
above Whitmore Wash

GRAND CANYON, ARIZONA
AUGUST, 15, 1969

60
Prickly pear fruit,
above Whitmore Wash

GRAND CANYON, ARIZONA
AUGUST 16, 1969

61

Waterfall
outside Travertine Grotto

GRAND CANYON, ARIZONA
SEPTEMBER 23, 1967

62

Side view of lower fall,
Travertine Falls

GRAND CANYON, ARIZONA
JUNE 29, 1967

63

Rocks at

Travertine Falls

GRAND CANYON, ARIZONA

JUNE 29, 1967

Appendix

Chronology

1901   Born in Winnetka, Illinois, December 6.

Before 1913   First photographs, of landscapes, using a Kodak box camera.

1913   Photographs birds on Great Spruce Head Island, Maine.

1920   Begins studying chemical engineering at Harvard University.

1924   Receives Bachelor of Science degree from Harvard Engineering School. Enrolls at Harvard Medical School.

1928   Marries Marian Brown.

1929   Awarded Doctor of Medicine degree from Harvard Medical School.

1929–1939   Works as a researcher and teacher of bacteriology and biological chemistry.

1930   Resumes photography after buying a Leica camera.

1931   Eliot, Jr., born, January 21.

1933   Charles Anthony born, December 24.

1934   Divorced.

1935   Photographic expedition to Switzerland and the Austrian Tyrol.

1936   Marries Aline Kilham.

1937   Stops photographing landscapes to concentrate on bird photography.

1938   Third son, Jonathan, born, March 25.

1939   Resigns from teaching to set up as a professional photographer, specializing in landscapes and wildlife.

Invents method for photographing birds in their natural habitat, using stroboscopic flashlights, blinds, scaffolds, and high ladders.

1940   Starts to specialize in color photography.

1941   Awarded a Guggenheim Fellowship to photograph birds in the U.S.

Fourth son, Stephen, born, July 23.

1942–1944   Employed in the Radiation Laboratory of the Massachusetts Institute of Technology, Boston.

1944   Returns to his birthplace.

1946   Moves to Santa Fe, New Mexico, where he will live for the rest of his life.

Patrick, his fifth son, born on February 4.

Becomes photographer-at-large for *Audubon Magazine*.

1949   Awarded another Guggenheim Fellowship to photograph birds.

1951   Photographs churches in Mexico.

1955–1956   Travels to Mexico, where he again photographs church architecture.

1960   Undertakes his first expedition to Glen Canyon, Utah, to which he will return in 1961, 1962, 1965, 1968, and 1971.

1963   Visits Adirondack Park, New York. Returns there in spring 1964 and in winter, spring, and fall 1965.

1964   From February to April visits Baja California, Mexico, to which he will return in July and August 1966.

1966   Travels to the Galápagos Islands, February to June.

1967   Travels to Greece and Turkey. Makes return visits in 1970 and 1971.

1968   Trip to Red River Gorge, Kentucky, on behalf of *Audubon Magazine*.

1969   Awarded Honorary Doctor of Fine Arts degree by Colby College, Waterville, Maine.

1970   Travels to Africa, February through November.

1972   Visits Iceland.

1973   Travels in Egypt in the spring and fall to photograph ancient monuments for E. P. Dutton & Company.

1974   Undertakes expedition to Antarctica, December through March 1975. Returns there December 1976 through March 1977.

1976   Spends the summer on Great Spruce Head Island, Maine, to which he will return in 1977, 1979, 1981, 1982, 1983, 1984, and 1986. Travels to Great Sand Dunes, Colorado, in September.

1977   Trip to Chaco Canyon, New Mexico.

1979   Spends March in Hawaii. Awarded an Honorary Doctor of Science degree from Dickinson College, Carlisle, Pennsylvania.

1981   Travels to China.

1982   Begins work on *Eliot Porter's Southwest*.

1985   Trip to Hong Kong and Macao in May, returning in June to Santa Fe.

1986   Spends his last summer on Great Spruce Head Island.

1990   Dies in Santa Fe, November 2.

Exhibition History

One-Man Shows

New York, Delphic Studios. February 24–March 8, 1936.

New York, An American Place. December 29, 1938–January 18, 1939. Traveled to Chicago, Georgia Lingafelt bookshop.

Santa Fe, Museum of New Mexico. March 15–30, 1940.

Chicago, Katharine Kuh Gallery. February 23–March 14, 1942.

New York, New York Zoological Society, Heads and Horns Gallery. May 30–June 30, 1942.

New York, The Museum of Modern Art. "Birds in Color: Flashlight Photographs by Eliot Porter." March 9–April 18, 1943. Circulated by the Smithsonian Institution Traveling Exhibition Service to twenty institutions, 1953–57.

Rochester, New York, George Eastman House. November–December 1951.

New York, Limelight Gallery. March 21–April 17, 1955.

New York, Limelight Gallery. "Madonnas and Marketplaces." April 4–May 19, 1957. Collaboration with Ellen Auerbach.

Santa Fe, Centerline General Store. "Mexican Baroque Church Art." June 15–August 15, 1957. Collaboration with Ellen Auerbach.

Santa Fe, Museum of New Mexico. July 1958. With Laura Gilpin.

Albuquerque, University of New Mexico. February 1–10, 1959.

Santa Fe, Centerline General Store. "The Seasons: A Photographic Essay." August 1–September 8, 1959.

Rochester, New York, George Eastman House.

"The Seasons: Color Photographs by Eliot Porter Accompanied by Quotations from Henry David Thoreau." August 12–October 1, 1960. Circulated by the Smithsonian Institution Traveling Exhibition Service to twenty-two institutions, 1960–64.

Chicago, Art Institute of Chicago. December 14, 1963–January 26, 1964.

San Francisco, M. H. de Young Memorial Museum. March 27–April 25, 1965.

New York, The Museum of Modern Art. "From the McAlpin Collection." December 14, 1966–February 12, 1967.

New York, Sierra Club Gallery. June 26–August 30, 1968.

Waterville, Maine, Colby College. "Photographs by Eliot Porter, Paintings by Fairfield Porter." May–June 1969.

San Francisco, Focus Gallery. "Thirty-Five Unpublished Pictures of Baja California and The Galápagos Islands." January 7–February 1, 1969.

Las Vegas, New Mexico, New Mexico Highlands University. January 4–30, 1970.

Phoenix, Arizona, Phoenix College. February 7–March 7, 1970.

Saint Petersburg, Florida, Museum of Fine Arts. March 15–April 15, 1970.

Princeton, New Jersey, the Art Museum, Princeton University. February 3–28, 1971.

New York, Neikrug Galleries. September 30–October 24, 1971.

Santa Fe, St. John's College. "Eliot Porter: Photographs of Classical Greece and Asia Minor; Aline Porter: Paintings." December 4–19, 1971.

Middletown, Connecticut, Wesleyan University, Davison Art Center. February 25–March 12, 1972.

Birmingham, Michigan, 831 Gallery. September 5–October 15, 1972.

Albuquerque, University of New Mexico. "The Eliot Porter Retrospective." March 20–April 15, 1973. Circulated by the University of New Mexico, 1973–75, and by the Western Association of Art Museums Traveling Exhibition Service, 1976–78.

Dallas, Texas, Afterimage Gallery. 1975.

Tacoma, Washington, Silver Image Gallery. February 4–March 2, 1975.

Boston, Harcus-Krakow-Rosen-Sonnabend Gallery. May 1975.

Worcester, Massachusetts, Worcester Art Museum. "Maine Photographs." December 16, 1975–March 7, 1976.

"Antarctica." With Daniel Lang. Circulated to eighteen locations by the Smithsonian Institution Traveling Exhibition Service, January 1976–February 1979.

Houston, Texas, Cronin Gallery. May 24–June 18, 1977.

Washington, D.C., Sander Gallery. "Mexican Church Interiors: Color Dye-transfers by Eliot Porter and Ellen Auerbach." September 30–October 28, 1978.

Birmingham, Michigan, Halstead 831 Gallery. January 9–February 10, 1979.

New York, The Metropolitan Museum of Art. "Intimate Landscapes." November 14, 1979–January 20, 1980.

Fort Worth, Texas, Amon Carter Museum. "Eliot Porter." October 31, 1987–January 3, 1988.

Group Exhibitions

New York, American Museum of Natural History. "The Fifth International Salon of Photography." April 14–28, 1938.

New York, The Museum of Modern Art. "Sixty Photographs." Winter 1939/40.

New York, American Museum of Natural History. "Seventh International Salon of Photography." March 6–29, 1940.

San Francisco, San Francisco Museum of Art. 1940.

New York, The Museum of Modern Art. "Image of Freedom." October 29, 1941–February 1, 1942.

New York, American Contemporary Art Gallery. "American Photography Today." July 31–August 31, 1944.

London, Central Hall, Westminster. "The Second Country Life International Exhibition of Wildlife Photographs." March 20–April 1, 1950.

Yosemite Valley, California, LeConte Lodge, and San Francisco, California Academy of Sciences. "This Is the American Earth." 1955. Circulated by the Smithsonian Institution Traveling Exhibition Service and by the United States Information Agency, April 1956–May 1957.

Santa Fe, Museum of New Mexico. "The First New Mexico Photographers Exhibition." June 17–July 14, 1956.

"I Hear America Singing." Circulated in Europe and the Middle East by the United States Information Agency, 1957.

"Volk aus vielen Völkern." Circulated in Germany by the United States Information Agency, 1957.

New York, The Metropolitan Museum of Art. "Photography in the Fine Arts I." May 1959.

Rochester, New York, George Eastman House. "Photography at Mid-Century." November 10, 1959–February 10, 1960.

New York, The Metropolitan Museum of Art. "Photography in the Fine Arts II." May 20–September 4, 1960.

New York, The Museum of Modern Art. "The Sense of Abstraction in Contemporary Photography." February 16–April 10, 1960.

Minneapolis, Minneapolis Institute of Arts. "Photography in the Fine Arts III." June 1961.

Lincoln, Massachusetts, DeCordova Museum. "Photography U.S.A. National Invitational Exhibition." January 28–March 18, 1962.

New York, The Metropolitan Museum of Art. "Photography in the Fine Arts IV." May 16–September 30, 1963.

New York, The Museum of Modern Art. "The Photographer and the American Landscape." September 24–November 28, 1963.

Northampton, Massachusetts, Smith College Museum of Art. "Spectrum." February 5–26, 1963. Traveled to eight institutions.

New Haven, Connecticut. Yale University Art Gallery. "Photography in America, 1850–1965." October 13–November 28, 1965.

Philadelphia, Philadelphia College of Art. "An Exhibition of Work by The John Simon Guggenheim Memorial Foundation Fellows in Photography." April 15–May 13, 1966.

Lincoln, Massachusetts, DeCordova Museum. "Photography U.S.A. '67." December 10, 1967–January 28, 1968.

Philadelphia, Philadelphia Museum of Art. "Selections from the Dorothy Norman Collection." May 24–September 1, 1968.

New York, The Metropolitan Museum of Art. "Landscape / Cityscape." November 13, 1973–January 6, 1974.

New York, Whitney Museum of American Art. "Photography in America." November 20, 1974–January 12, 1975.

Wellesley, Massachusetts, Wellesley College Museum. "Color Photography Now." September 29–October 27, 1975.

London, Victoria and Albert Museum. "The Land: Twentieth-Century Landscape Photographs." November 12, 1975–February 15, 1976. Traveled to five museums in Great Britain.

St. Louis, University of Missouri art gallery. "Aspects of American Photography 1976." April 1–30, 1976.

Boulder, University of Colorado. "The Great West: Real / Ideal." September 10–October 15, 1977.

New York, The Metropolitan Museum of Art. "The Collection of Alfred Stieglitz: Fifty Pioneers of Modern Photography." May 18–July 16, 1978.

New York, The Museum of Modern Art. "Mirrors and Windows: American Photography since 1960." July 28–October 2, 1978.

Albuquerque, University of New Mexico Art Museum. "The History of Photography in New Mexico." April 1–July 29, 1979.

Books of Photographs by Eliot Porter

In Wildness Is the Preservation of the World. San Francisco: Sierra Club, 1962.

The Place No One Knew: Glen Canyon on the Colorado. San Francisco: Sierra Club, 1963.

Forever Wild: The Adirondacks. Blue Mountain Lake, N.Y.: Adirondack Museum, and New York: Harper & Row, 1966.

Summer Island: Penobscot Country. San Francisco: Sierra Club, 1966.

Baja California and the Geography of Hope, with Joseph Wood Krutch. San Francisco: Sierra Club, 1967.

Galápagos: The Flow of Wildness. San Francisco: Sierra Club, 1968.

Down the Colorado. New York: E. P. Dutton, 1969.

Appalachian Wilderness: The Great Smoky Mountains, with Edward Abbey. New York: E. P. Dutton, 1970.

Birds of North America: A Personal Selection. New York: E. P. Dutton, 1972.

The Tree Where Man Was Born: The African Experience, with Peter Matthiessen. New York: E. P. Dutton, 1972.

Moments of Discovery: Adventures with American Birds, with Michael Harwood. New York: E. P. Dutton, 1977.

Antarctica. New York: E. P. Dutton, 1978.

Intimate Landscapes. New York: The Metropolitan Museum of Art, 1979.

The Greek World, with Peter Levi. New York: E. P. Dutton, 1980.

American Places, with Wallace Stegner. New York: E. P. Dutton, 1981.

All Under Heaven: The Chinese World, with Jonathan Porter. New York: Pantheon Books, 1983.

Eliot Porter's Southwest. New York: Holt, Rinehart, and Winston, 1985.

Maine. Boston: Little, Brown, 1986.

Eliot Porter. Boston: Little, Brown, 1987.

Mexican Churches, with Ellen Auerbach. Albuquerque: University of New Mexico Press, 1987.

The West. New York: New York Graphic Society, 1988.

Iceland, with Jonathan Porter. Boston: Little, Brown, 1989.

Mexican Celebrations, with Ellen Auerbach. Albuquerque: University of New Mexico Press, 1990.

Monuments of Egypt, with Wilma Stern. Albuquerque: University of New Mexico Press, 1990.

Nature's Chaos, with James Gleick. New York: Viking, 1990.